Chue is pronounced CHEW. It means *bell* and can be a name for a girl or a boy.

Dawb is pronounced DUH, with a rising tone. It means *white* and can be a name for a girl or a boy.

Hmong is pronounced MOHNG. The word refers to a people, an ethnic minority, from Southeast Asia. Starting in 1975, many Hmong families came to the United States as refugees of war.

Lei is pronounced LAY. It is a name for a girl or a boy.

me naib is pronounced MEE NYE with a rising tone at the end. It is a term of endearment for a child, similar to "my dear" or "my darling."

phim nyu vais is pronounced PEE NYU VYE. The word refers to an evil spirit that causes sickness and death.

pog ntxoog is pronounced BAH TXHONG. The word refers to a female jungle spirit who was once human and is the size of a child.

For the everlasting beauty of a grandmother's smile. For Youa Lee, the
grandma in this book, and Joua Thao, the grandma I never got to meet but
whose love shines through my mother.
—K.K.Y.

For Grandma, who forgot everything but will never be forgotten
—K.L.

Carolrhoda Books®
An imprint of Lerner Publishing Group, Inc.
241 First Avenue North
Minneapolis, MN 55401 USA

For reading levels and more information, look up this title at www.lernerbooks.com.

Designed by Emily Harris.
Main body text set in Horley Old Style MT Std Semibold. Typeface provided by Monotype Typography.
The illustrations in this book were created with mixed media and Photoshop.

Library of Congress Cataloging-in-Publication Data

Names: Yang, Kao Kalia, 1980– author. | Le, Khoa, 1982– illustrator.
Title: The most beautiful thing / Kao Kalia Yang ; illustrated by Khoa Le.
Description: Minneapolis : Carolrhoda Books®, 2020. | Audience: Ages 5–9 | Audience: Grades 2–3 | Summary:
   "Drawn from Kao Kalia Yang's childhood experiences as a Hmong refugee, this heartfelt picture book offers a
   window into the life of a family with little money and a great deal of love"— Provided by publisher.
Identifiers: LCCN 2019050935 (print) | LCCN 2019050936 (ebook) | ISBN 9781541561915 (library binding) |
   ISBN 9781541599376 (ebook)
Subjects: LCSH: Immigrant families—United States—Juvenile literature. | Grandparent and child—United States—
   Juvenile literature.
Classification: LCC JV6475 .Y36 2020 (print) | LCC JV6475 (ebook) | DDC 305.8959/72073—dc23

LC record available at https://lccn.loc.gov/2019050935
LC ebook record available at https://lccn.loc.gov/2019050936

Manufactured in the United States of America
5-51677-47486-9/9/2021

The Most Beautiful Thing

Kao Kalia Yang

Illustrated by **Khoa Le**

Carolrhoda Books • Minneapolis

My grandmother is so old, no one knows how old she is.

Not me, not my big sister Dawb, not our older cousin Lei.

My father waits patiently when we try to guess her age.
He is my grandma's ninth and youngest child, and even
he does not know how old she is.

We know that my grandma was born on the other side of the world, across a wide ocean.

My grandma came from a time and a place where creatures lurked in the jungles waiting to chase unwary children. She told us that she once looked into the gleaming eyes of a tiger and felt its hot breath on her face.

By the time I was born, my grandmother already had an old woman's face. Her skin was soft but dry like paper and in her mouth was a single tooth.

Grandma said, "It is the only thing standing strong in my mouth, this final tooth that my mother and father gave me."

I asked to see a picture of her parents.

She said, "Me naib, they lived in a time long
before the Hmong learned of such things as
photographs." She pointed to her heart, "The
only picture I have of them is here."

The luckiest of the grandchildren got to help take care of Grandma.

Lei got to wash Grandma's clothes by hand at the bathroom sink with sweet-smelling pink soap.

Dawb got to wash Grandma's soft brown back in the bathtub with a soapy cloth.

And me? I got to clip her fingernails and toenails while Grandma sat on her favorite stool in the light from the window.

I can still feel the roughness of Grandma's heels in my hand, the thickness of her toenails in between my fingers. I can see the bottoms of her feet, thick and brown and broken, deep cracks filled with dirt from long ago and far away.

Grandma told me that her mother and father
died when she was a little girl.

Grandma was just a child herself, but she had
to take care of her two younger brothers and
baby sister.

I looked up at my grandma from the place
where I sat at her feet, and I asked her, "How
did you get food for them?"

Grandma said, "I didn't find enough food.
We lived always with hunger eating us on
the inside."

All my life with her, even with just her one
tooth, Grandma never said no when we
offered her something to eat.

The ice cream truck was singing its song
from down the street. I looked underneath
the couch for quarters. There were none.
So I got ice cubes from the freezer.

I offered one to Grandma
in my red plastic cup.
She smiled at me.

When I wanted a new dress to wear on the first day of third grade, my mother said she did not have enough money. She found some nickels and a dime in her purse and offered them to me.

I bought hard peppermint candies from the
neighborhood grocery at the corner of our block.
When I got home, I offered one to Grandma on
the palm of my hand. She smiled at me.

At the round table with its shaky legs, I used my spoon to mix and mix in the center soup bowl we all shared. There were no pieces of meat, only bones, and soft greens.

My father said, "The price of meat is too expensive at the market, me naib."

I found a thick chunk of bone and offered it to Grandma on my spoon. She smiled at me.

We had plenty of meat only when we celebrated
Hmong New Year with our aunts, uncles, and
cousins. The old table was heavy with whole, boiled
chickens, more than our family could ever eat. After
dinner, our bellies full, my cousins and I sat on the
carpet around Grandma as she told us stories.

She always began, "It was a long time ago and I was
just a girl . . ."

As we listened, our eyes grew round. Grandma twisted her fingers, one over the other, to show us what the hands of *poj ntxoog*, jungle spirits the size of children, looked like. She taught us how to listen for the cries of the fearsome *phim nyu vais* by holding our breath until our hearts pounded in our ears.

We were always sad when Aunt Chue called, "Time for the children to help clean up!"

On a cold day, when the snow blew onto the windowpanes and the light was dim, I asked Grandma about the dirt in her feet.

She told me she didn't have shoes after her mother and father died. She went shoeless to the mountains to tend to the family field. She ventured into the jungle to look for wild roots, bamboo shoots, and edible mushrooms. And one day, she was chased by a tiger—as she fled, her bare feet broke open on the fallen branches, and she still ran, blood and dirt mixing into clay with each step.

I squeezed her feet in my arms and pulled them close to my heart, a hug for the hard road she's walked to get to me.

Each year, cutting my grandma's nails went
faster because I grew stronger and bigger and
more able. Each year, Grandma's feet felt
smaller and smaller in my hands and my lap.

Her stories, too, slowed with the passing years.
The pauses between her words grew long.